DELUSION CONFUSION COLLUSION

WHO TRUMP WHO

TRINIDAD MOLINA

TMJ Publishing

Paperback ISBN: 978-0-578-22868-6
Hardback ISBN: 978-0-578-22869-3

PRINTED IN THE UNITED STATES OF AMERICA

Introduction

WE LIVE IN a country that has given us certain freedoms and liberties and the right to be happy in our persons. There have been many who have tried to change our way of life. in the same token many have defended our way of life, for more than two hundred years we have lived a life that was given to us by non-other than our God. You may or may not know this, but this great nation was founded on biblical principles that some of us so dearly cherish. Our Ivey league Universities and schools were created to educate our people on the word of God. This was the basic reason for education in those early days. What has happened since? was the separation of Church and State, but this was not supposed to have happened when this was enforced, we kick God out of our Schools and not long after that we kicked him out of our everyday life. The constitution says we are to worship God how we see fit. There is nothing in the constitution that says we should not worship God. Our founding Fathers had a strong belief in the almighty God. They also knew that if they remained in his word, they would be prosperous and successful. Many christians in the early days sacrificed their life for what they believed. Today we must ever be so vigilant and watchful of who wants to make their dwelling in these United States of America. Because God has blessed this nation Many people from many nations want to make this land their home. what they are looking for is Life, Liberty and the pursuit of property these things are what many look for. We have also been infiltrated by those who would like nothing more than to destroy what this nation had stood for, for many years or should I say since the colonizing of the North American Continent. I must remind you, because this nation was a nation under God. We were prosperous and successful. I look around today, and what I see is we have moved away from being a nation under God. These United States as we know it will destroy itself. and that's exactly what will happen. The only way to avoid such a catastrophe. We must get this nation back under God or suffer the consequences. Are we really that blind or are we just refusing to acknowledge God our creator and savior? Are We Headed for an Economic and Political collapse? Do we not see with our own eyes what is really happening? The divisiveness between our own people, the lies that have been created by our own government and the movement to rid ourselves from a democracy that was established when we became a nation under God. let us all get back under God. Today, the stage is being set for this precious nation to be destroyed by those who only care for themselves and not give a hoot who they hurt along the way. The Ideology of some of those people who are running for office has been changed it is not what this nation was founded on. Some of our citizens have drifted away from their own Ideology and own beliefs and have decided to follow what is a lie and that could destroy our nation as we know it. let all Americans of this nation who are Christian unite together and get on our knees in prayer and ask God for His forgiveness and He will forgive us. Let us avoid our own demise before it's too late. Let us get back to the basics of Love, because God is "LOVE"

Chapter One

As I was laying on the couch this morning just watching my favorite news Channel which is Fox and Friends. Here, where I live, this news cast starts at 5:am and as I'm looking at what is going on in the world today, I can't help but wonder how did we get where we are today? As I ponder these thoughts It makes me think of all my unfortunate troubles I've been through and there have been many. In my walk-through life I have met many people some good and some not so good. God has given me so far 60 years of life and still going strong thank you Jesus. Its been a journey that is still in process. What has been going on all these years? Where have we gone wrong, or is there more to come? I can remember as far back as four years of age playing in the park with my sister and getting a foot full of those grass stickers well that's what I call them anyway they hurt so much. I remember crying and wanting to go home. It was a rather strange and very painful event in my life. I also know that my father was an immigrant from Mexico and after being in the United States he applied and became an American citizen. We never were middle class or High-class citizens, but we managed the best we could. Both my parents worked to put food on the table and pay whatever bills they had pending. There were times we couldn't even afford Christmas gifts like some people did but so what we were alive and doing O.K. There were times we did not have anything, like other kids did, but we always had the little food my dad would bring home from the odd jobs he did. I'm sure there are a lot of families who did the same thing we did to make ends meet. My brothers and sisters started to work at a very young age to help put food on the table and help pay what bills we needed to pay. I can remember at the age of eight I was already shining shoes and selling newspapers house to house in the neighborhood, I also sold fresh vegetables and fruits door to door you know the same as I did the newspaper to make money to help out. since we couldn't afford much. I learned at an early age about the value of money and and what it is to be frugal at times. I grew up with both my parents living at home with 12 children to feed and cloth, it wasn't easy at all. We grew up in the housing projects in Texas and that's because that was all my parents could afford, they never were homeowners so we never new what it felt to have your own home. My mother only had a third-grade education just as well as my dad. my father, he was a very responsible, hard working man. My parents were very strict. They knew the dangers that were prevalent in the neighborhood. I guess that's why they kept a close eye on us when we were school aged children it's also the reason they always wanted to know with whom we were associating with or who we had as friends, as we grew older and, well, being typical kids we did do some things that did not go to well with our parents, so we suffered the consequences and boy did we ever.

Even though we grew up in the housing projects we all graduated high school. The years for me growing up were fun and exciting to say the least. And as life moves ahead, we all grow up and became men and women. As I look back at some of those people I grew up with some are still living and some are either dead or in and out of prisons, some are even still in prison for life and just as it was in our neighborhood some have become drug Addicts, and then as it is with life, Some have gone on and made good for themselves. For me I married young. Deep down inside me I was holding on to a shameful secret you see I was violated when I was just eight years old, and never told a soul about what had happened to me It was all just bottled up inside me. As I grew up it was laying heavy on my mind and I continued to keep this inside of me for as long as I could.. When I reached the age I could drink I found this was just the thing I needed to hide my shame, and these were the times when I drank like a fish. I drank so much that within my own family and so-called friends I was treated as a pariah. The time came when I had no place to call home, and so I wondered from town to town, city to city all this began to happen just after my marriage fell apart, but non the less it happened to me. I soon found myself homeless, I really thought at times that I would die in some sidewalk somewhere on skid row, but I guess God had other plans for me. As a homeless man I met many homeless people just as myself there were some whom I could Identify with because those were the ones who were going through the same set of circumstances as myself and because of our adversities(troubles) we understood each other. I made my home in men's shelters, underpasses, in the bushes on the town side walks and sometimes parks. I did what was expected of me if I wanted to stay in the bushes with other homeless people. I had to bring in money for our group like panhandle or hold a sign out in the street asking for donations to contribute my share of responsibility. As a homeless man I talked to many homeless men and women and found out all kinds of reasons why one becomes homeless and believe it or not some homeless people are homeless because they want to be homeless they don't want the responsibility of being accountable for things and they like it just fine. Others are homeless due to uncontrollable conditions. the elderly who are homeless, are homeless because some families don't want the responsibility of caring for their elderly relatives, so these people are thrown out on the street to fend for themselves. And then there are those with mental Illnesses who are societies unwanted and discarded individuals. Then you have those homeless who are wanted by the law they figure they can hide within the homeless people, but the law always manages to catch-up with them. Some are just hiding and pretending to be homeless they really don't want to be found or bothered by life's problems and they are comfortable that way. I never did stay in any one place for long, or hung around with a group of people. It was in this time in my life that I started to listen to the news and get into heated discussion with people about the world we live in. I educated myself in different areas of studies. When I was growing up, I did not care about what was going on in the world. I only cared about me little did I know that what happens politically effects everyone even in some small way. I read many books and became more aware of the politics involve in every walk of life. I was a democrat because my parents were democrats, I change my affiliation when I started reading and looking at the issues more closely. Today I have a whole different way of thinking. My parents have since gone from this life. As a young child I can still remember when John F. Kennedy was assassinated in 1963 my mother was hanging laundry on the cloth line when the television program was interrupted with the special report about President Kennedy being shot.

It was a day of sadness for the whole country. I saw my mother crying and wondering why she is crying? so I asked her, and she told me in Spanish "because they just killed one of the finest president that ever took office," well that might have been I saw the news which was constantly reporting the Vietnam conflict. In that point in time since then there have been many good candidates who were elected president. While I was growing up. I saw on television vice president Johnson as he was being sworn in as president of the United States. During those times I saw news which was constantly reporting news of the Vietnam conflict. I can remember it well because of all the riots and protest airing in the news. The nation was also divided then too. It was a time when my eldest brother was drafted to fight in Vietnam. While serving his country he received the purple heart for an injury he received while on the front. I can remember Nixon winning the presidency and his downfall. Which made way for President Gerald Ford to take office. In the news they announce the end of the Vietnam War; The most undeserved thing about this conflict was how we treated our fighting heroes, when they arrived home the nation was very disrespectful and so malicious.

CHAPTER TWO

TODAY I HAVE great respect for these men who fought in this war I salute all of you. Well I was just a kid at that time; but I saw many wrongs that were made back then, just as they are being made today. Now that I'm a grown man and read a lot and studied a lot I have a better understanding of things. While I was in high school, we were taught about history from the first colony and the wars that were fought to get our freedom. The civil war all the way through the constitution. We were taught about slavery and the many African Americans contributed and fought for there freedom. While I was in prison, I was amazed at how many people have no clue what party Abraham Lincoln was affiliated with and now for those who don't know. President Lincoln was a Republican. It was a Republican who was against slavery and he saw fit to set them free because they too deserved dignity and respect, so he set them free.

The outcome of President Lincolns life, he was assassinated by an Ignorant assassin. What President Lincoln wanted was the best for all men. I'm sure Lincoln had strong opposition towards his proclamation of Emancipation back when he first made it known to his congressional colleagues. So, don't forget this Republican paid the ultimate price for wanting to do good for all men. President Lincoln never gave in to the ridicules and bad mouthing he received for his decisions. In todays political rhetoric we are more concern about absolutely nothing of Importance as we were in historical times. Why is it in America the land of the free and the brave feel that we have to be politically correct and try not to offend or step on anybody's toes, to me that's just full of dung(s***) We need to get over that stuff. As I had mention before I used to be a democrat and that was just because my parents were democrats. This also included my religious beliefs I was a catholic because my parents were Catholics all these affiliations were not by choice, I was born into them so to I was born into poverty. My inner light started to become brighter when I was twelve years old I became a born again Christian I learned things from the bible that really opened up my intellect I began to ask questions in school some of my classmate would make fun of me or would literally threaten me with physical harm if I would ask more than one question. It didn't bother me that I was being threaten I was hungry for answers, so I asked. after a few years it all just wasn't important anymore. The people I started hanging around with were very different and my interest were also different, because now I was in Junior high (middle School is what they call it now) it was a time of growing up and change. I started hanging around with a bunch of pot heads back then, even though we were all friends and they did their marijuana smoking before going to class I myself never touched the stuff there was peer pressure, but I had a strong fear for drug use I would always refused and one of the greatest reason for this fear was of the horror stories I have heard while growing up about how kids were becoming addicted to stronger drugs after just trying marijuana so I never took any interest in wanting to even try it for kicks. and my friends never would force it on me. In school I was a popular student and sometimes the class clown. It was a time when the word politically correct was non-existent today we find ourselves walking on egg shells making sure we don't insult anyone or any establishment what is all that about? we're not what it used to be; many changes have come around and to me one of the greatest changes ever made was the day we took God out of our lives and out of our schools. We have completely made Him of no value in our life as we had before. I got news for all of you God is still sitting on his throne and looking at us. We as a nation used to be under God, now we've become a nation over God. I remember growing up in the housing projects we still had respect for our elderly, our neighbor, as a young man we also had respect for the ladies. Today we get so offended by what somebody said while expressing their opinions we must get pass those ridiculous feelings. As a human being we all have our own opinions and we must respect each other's opinions and not take it too personal. While in prison I've seen altercations for what someone said or made an opinion of a subject and the other person took it as an offense. As I grew up it was a most difficult of times that I had to work at an early age to help put food on the table by the age of nine I was already shining shoes selling news papers selling fruits and vegetables door to door in my neighborhood it wasn't easy but we manage well. My father was a very strict father and a disciplinarian, in those day's we could not express our opinions if we did well let's just say we had it bad for a few minutes. As I have said we all have opinions and our beliefs.

It was when I grew up a little that I started to realize my parents beliefs were not what I wanted to believe. I was a democrat because my parents were democrats I was also a catholic because they were Catholics and for a long time I had the same thoughts that they did and as I said I started to educate myself and forming my own beliefs and Ideals. Today I'm a republican by choice and I'm also a born-again Christian. When I was 12 years of age, I got involve with the church not the catholic church but a Christian church it was the best years of my life that I had growing up. As for my parents they had their own beliefs, take for instance my father, he did not believe in God at least I don't think he did by some of his comments he mad about certain people and his way of thinking. I can remember the day when the Apollo astronauts first landed on the moon. When my dad saw that we were all watching the event as it unfolded through the television my dad said that all that was not real it was all a put on by the government that this show was being filmed somewhere out in the desert to make it look like they were on the moon it was all Hollywood made. At the time we started to believe our parents it was pathetic if you ask me. Well today I know better. This nation has come along way and of course mistakes were mad along the way. Today this so called politically correct thing is dividing this nation more and more each day. What is starting to happen as I write these lines some of our citizens in several cities have started to ask government officials to remove some of those statues that are representative of what this nation has gone through, whether good or bad, some serve as a reminder of the errors that were made back then and the sacrifices our heroes made to make this nation what it is today they have started taking our history away how else are our children suppose to know what happens if we go a certain direction. Do we also stop teaching history to our children and let them go through life not knowing how this nation suffered throughout these years? I really hate to see this happen to our future leaders. To be politically correct is not what we are all about we are much better than that. Do these organization really believe they are helping our nation by doing the things they do; to me what it does is gets us more divided than you can imagine. Whatever happened to those words that ring so sweet "one nation under God Indivisible" (Incapable of being divided.) What we need is to go back to basics of history and find where we went wrong I've given you my opinion as to what might have gone awry or wrong but look at it for yourself and lets start to live our life as we should without hate or prejudices knowing that I have an open mind and I am willing to hear your opinions because we are all alike on the inside. We all come from different countries but we are all the same there is no such thing as race because nobody has a different color skin look closely we are all brown colored skin there are no white people or yellow people or black people we are all brown some are a lighter brown than others and some are darker brown than others there is only one race the human race it was mans ignorance that gave us these racial classes but with all respect for all people we are really the same color as the old saying goes if you cut anyone person they will inevitably bleed red. What we have are different cultures and beliefs and that is what makes each one of us special, So, stop the hate. When have you ever read in the bible where Jesus called anyone by the color of their skin? never then why should we classify them in such matter Jesus called them by where they were from like Mary Magdalene her name was Mary and she was from Magdalen, Just like Leonardo De Vinci his name was Leonardo from De Vinci. Magdalen and De Vinci were not their last names

It was where they were from. The list goes on why man in his in-finite wisdom decided to put colors on people that's just tells me its man's own ignorance that stands out and in todays world more so than any other time. This type of classification has stuck to us through many years. And there's more to our naming people say for instance on immigration we call those people who are from a distant land or country aliens why? let me just say why are we comparing them to extraterrestrial or from outer space these are people just like you and me in my book they are foreigners and the bible describes them as so. Where in the bible do you hear or read the word aliens? We insult people without being aware that it's happening.

Chapter Three

WHILE I WAS in prison I made many observations that really did not make any sense at all; like this one, Inmates who were of the same culture insulted each other using words that if any other culture used them this would be offensive to them but yet they use it all the time why would you find something so offensive when you yourselves are using these same words to relate to each other this was just so hypocritical I had to ask why would he use such language to his own people and yet get offended when others are using the same language? and this wasn't the only thing I observed while I was incarcerated. I had spent six years with people and I mean this word was not only aimed at a specific culture but mostly everybody used it and this was the "F" word it was probably the most used word in the system by both inmates and guards or TDCJ employees. What I found out was many were so used to using this word it just came as a natural word for them I guess they didn't know any other words than that word which I found very irritating and offensive I would often make it known to those whom were using the word in every sentence how terrible their vocabulary was using this word. As I mention earlier,

I grew up in the same type of neighborhood as most of these inmates and I had no use for this word at all. I also learned that this popular word would almost always lead to an altercation. In prison I use to wake up early in the morning to catch my favorite news cast which was "Fox and Friends" I found this news cast to be very informative and honest when I first got to prison I use to see the other regular news cast until I started to realize how there hatred has caused many followers to do the same I came across Fox and Friends one morning while I was awake by myself and notice how honest and informative this news cast was and that is how I got hooked on this channel this was even before Donald Trump was even president. A lot of what happened in prison is written in my other book called "The Twisted System." Well as the prison days went on I started to make comparisons between those other news cast and the one I have chosen as my favorite it was during the election night that really just made me more glad that I was a republican and not a democrate. As I listened to these popular or so called popular news coverage of the election I notice they didn't want Donald Trump to win they were rooting for Hillary Clinton to win. It was during the election coverage that I got my first look at the bias the regular news cast was, and how unfair they treated Donald Trump. It could have been while he was just a candidate, but I guess the hatred for Donald Trump became more obvious on election night. I also saw this hatred in some of the inmates when they knew Donald Trump had won the Presidency. I went through a time of ridicule and contempt while I was in prison, I guess everyone in my dorm knew my affiliation because I never kept it a secret if anyone ask what my political affiliation was, I would let them know.

and as a republican in prison with no gang affiliation this could have been a lot more challenging. I was called all kinds of names, but I never took it personal I just let them vent out whatever it was they wanted to get off their chest. This went on for about a week or two some wanted to know why I was in favor of Donald Trump being president the first thing that came to mind was Donald Trump is not a politician and he's more of a businessman like me. I heard so many negative things about Mr. Trump that were not true and what I would question was where you heard this from and always the answer would be from ABC, CNN, MSNBC and all those other stations. The next question I would ask would be did you hear him yourself? and the answer there would always be well yea it was in the news then I would watch the news with these people and yes they were showing Mr. Trump talking but they were editing what was being said and not all of the story was shown they would show only what they wanted the public to see or hear never the complete story. Then I would tell them why are you listening to garbage that is not even the whole story your looking at what they want you to see or hear. I would go on to explain what was said on the Fox News and It was completely different than what was on the other channels it took awhile to convince them about the truth and to have an open mind towards everything they hear or see. After watching the elections and found out that Donald Trump had just been elected President all hell broke loose in my dorm. I couldn't help but smile at all the idiotic things that were being said from my fellow inmates nobody was happy, but maybe three of four of us out of the sixty eight inmates who were in the same dorm that I was in. that night I slept with one eye open or lets just say I had very little sleep. The following day it was business as usual in the prison unit I was housed in, and we went about our day as we always did. When time came for the news to come on it was a

DELUSION CONFUSION COLLUSION

very strange and different kind of news. These news cast had people on their news cast making all kinds of erroneous predictions and opinions about how Donald Trump is unfit to be president he has no experience being president when I heard that comment I thought to myself nobody who has ever been elected president really has any experience in this high position it is a position of learn as you go this is the reason you select your advisors and counselors to guide you and to be there for you. "The economy is going to suffer because of Trump's presidency." I also heard things like Trumps not fit to be president! They tried so hard to make Trump look so bad it was pathetic. For the next month or so things were still the same I mean every talk show and every media outlet was just out to degrade our President elect Donald Trump. Why was the hate so strong I just couldn't understand the media nor the people who spoke on these shows giving their opinions on subjects they themselves probably know nothing about. The only channel that was ever fair and honest was the fox and friends news cast so from what I was listening to in the regular news cast just turned me off completely and I found the news that to me was not bias but sincere and to the point. At some point in time news broke out that the Russians had a hand on the elections and boy all hell broke loose the word colluding was being said everywhere for those who don't know colluding means here's the meaning from (Oxford English Dictionary)"Make a secret plan with someone to do something illegal or dishonest." The democratic Party was accusing the Russian government of hacking into their computers and making all kinds of horrible things and that's why Hillary Clinton lost.

I mean they came with some of the most outrageous things just to discredit the election process and because they could not except the fact that Donald Trump had been elected by most people who went out to vote. When the news broke out about the so called "collusion Theory" during all this guessing by the democratic party many of these inmates kept coming to me and asking me what was happening and what is this word "collusion" that keeps coming up and I would explain to them as best as possible but most of these inmates had already formed an opinion by what they heard in the regular news cast. This is only an opinion of what I thought when all this was going on It was a ploy by the democratic party to get the heat off of Hillary Clinton and her E-mail problems this I believe was the main objective of this whole "Collusion Theory" Why they didn't want Hillary to look bad in publics eye. The e-mail problems weren't the only problem plaguing Hillary Clinton there was the "Benghazi" Situation that needed to be accounted for, what happened at Benghazi? In 2012 when Hillary ran against Obama, she also lost that election and for the likes of me it was not a spectacle as the lost she endured to Donald Trump. I guess the lost of the election to Donald Trump took a toll on Hillary Clinton and many of her followers that she totally secluded herself for a while and did not make any appearances nor did she want people to know what was going on, to me I felt she had taken the lose a little to hard I supposed even the Democratic party took it very hard because the hatred toward Donald Trump became even greater it was so great a hatred that the Democratic party and the media started putting out wild stories against Donald Trump and his campaign. One of the biggest and most dense stories was about the secret meeting between Trump and Russia joining together to commit a crime which is called "colluding" this to me was all made up to try to get him impeached many people are involve in this investigation that was started by the haters of Trump who were and are in a position of power. These people have gone to the extreme of making up Documents against Trump called a "Dossier" this even involves judges and lawyers and F.B.I agents who were in position of authority these Trump nemeses wanted him out of office. The left went so far as to hire a special counsel to investigate this so-called meeting with Trump and the Russian Government. What has happened was that during this so-called collusion investigation the lives of two people were forever changed because of their affiliation with Donald Trump These two people were charged with charges not related to the collusion investigation. Well since nothing was happening with the collusion investigation stories start to come out of the wood about what President Trump did sixteen years earlier, do I really want to know what he did sixteen years earlier with his personal life? No!! I want to know what he's doing right now as President. No matter how bad things looked for Donald Trump he always maintained his Character and dignity in public, grant you the man is not a politician so he may have been a little rough around the edges and during his campaign he made certain promises, and has so far kept his word you can't ask for a better politician or person than the one the majority voted for and elected. This man has kept his word as president of these United States I can proudly say this man is a man of Character when it comes to being President of our great nation God Bless him. When all of these accusations against Donald Trump were being made I was reminded of the story in the bible about the adulteress when Jesus told the crowd of hypocrites "He who is without sin cast the first stone." nobody was left to throw the first stone.

Nevertheless, the left has and is doing the best they can to stop Donald Trump from succeeding in his Presidency. While I was in prison, I had to defend myself for why I believed the way I did both in Jesus Christ and in Donald Trump. I have had very strong arguments for my belief and for the most part I would make them look at things with an open mind. One of my biggest defenses was what has Obama done for his people? and after a few thoughtful moments the answer would be "Nothing" then because they were not to fond of republicans my next question to them would be you all know who freed the slaves right? well did you know that President Lincoln was a Republican? many were surprise to hear Lincoln was a republican. It is my belief that the democrats want to keep you in slavery still. I'll explain this observation later. but these were my defense. I have always stood my ground for what I believe in.

Chapter Four

I DON'T WATCH the regular news anymore because of all the hatred they have spread through out this country of ours they say that President Donald Trump has divided this nation and have called him a liar but if the public would really look at who really are the dividers of our lovely nation you will see for yourself who they really are who are dividing our nation. Let's examine our previous President before Donald Trump the democrat's wonderful commander and chief Barrack Obama. What did he do for our country and for the people of America and I do mean all races of people who are American Citizens whether born or nationalized? I myself can not find one thing he has done that has made our country a better place to live. As I have said before this nation was a nation under God when did it become a nation over God? I guess It happened when God was taken out of our schools and out of our lives this was done in my belief out of misinterpreting the U.S. Constitution.

You can argue all you want about the constitution, but God is still God. The liberal party is now having a field day, now that God is out of the picture and so they want all kinds of laws passed that would satisfy their own desires and wants they are probably saying no God no accountability for our sins. But that's for another date and time today let's deal with what's at hand Donald Trump wants to make America great again and I know he is doing a very good job at what he promised during the campaign. whatever happened to the money President Obama gave the Iranians I saw pellets of money being handed over to the Iranian government and it was all cash why has no one ever say anything about that deal? or why did Obama released vicious and top terrorist leaders from Guantanamo bay Cuba? some of these terrorists have returned to what they were taught to do and that is to behead and kill innocent people how could this happen and better yet why did this happened where was Pelosi and Schumer why did they not release non-violent criminals who are American citizens Obama released some in 2009 and then he did it again years later and then before he left office this just boggles the mind. As I see it he did more for other countries like those who back these terrorist and those terrorist themselves, while Americans prisoners who are non violent sit in prison for life but it's OK to release vicious criminals who would like nothing more than to kill Americans now what's wrong with this picture? It could be therefore he received the "Noble Peace Prize" after all Obama received it for his contribution for the efforts to strengthen International Diplomacy and cooperation between people. Well I don't really know, but it sure is questionable. President Bush also release prisoners from Guantanamo Bay Cuba, and he should not have done that what a stupid mistake on both parties. To me these were very disturbing I guess nobody has ever question anything Obama did regardless of how bad it looked. Was what he did part of his executive authority which follows what is in the constitution right? Whatever bad thing Obama did back then when he was president was just another day at the office. Obama could do no wrong and if I can let my mind wonder I can just see Pelosi and Schumer with pom poms cheering him on "Obama! Obama! he's our man" I heard Obama once say that the economy was getting better before he left office. Is that true? well I did some looking back at the economy when I got out of prison and what I found out is Mr. Obama is wrong the economy was not at all in a recovery here's what I found through google dot com. According to the news from google they don't know how the economy was holding on because people were unemployed the rate was at 7.7 percent and this was only for those who were reported as unemployed there were many others who were not counted because they had given up on finding a jobs so Obama again did nothing to get the economy moving but yet he's giving away pellets of money to those who support terrorist. Its my opinion President Obama does not deserve the noble peace prize he should be in prison for aiding and abetting known terrorist and enemies' of the state that's just my belief. Why did this stupidity happen because if Nancy Pelosi and Schumer were in office, they looked the other way when it involves a democrat that's what my observation has been and continues to happen? When I was in prison there were few people who told me they were in there for a crime they did not commit just like myself and yet President Obama and President Bush are releasing the enemy what happened the oath of office they swore to defend? To me they must have lied with their hand on the Bible. and then after some time Mr. McNab appeared on the 60 minutes show where he is disclosing all that was happening and how both of them wanted to remove our newly elected President Donald Trump and this is what they are calling it a "coup" I believe deep down these two agents should be serving time in federal prison with stiff sentences for what they were doing in secret along with all those involved. These Federal agents also take an oath of office to protect our country and its citizens in my opinion this is nothing more than treason and wanting to over throw the presidency why are they still free its as if the democrats are turning a blind eye to the truth where is justice being fair? I'm sure there will be more to come out if they are put before a panel who investigates these things. Well this is all I have to say look at President Donald Trump and look at President Barrack Obama there is no comparison President Donald Trump is a far better President than Bush and Obama put together by far. And the people together with the so called "Fake" news have the gall to treat President Trump with disdain you ought to be proud we have a President who keeps his promises and does them no matter how many people ridicules him. one thing for sure he's got the American peoples back no matter who you are, Thank You President Trump.

The GDP was at 2.2 percent again another error on behalf of Obama. Today as I look back at the Obama years and the now elected President Donald Trump, we as a nation are doing a lot better than the previous President who insists on taking credit where it is not due. The Bible says "give credit where credit is due" In my honest opinion President Obama did more for the terrorist than he did for his country I might be wrong but its pretty hard to see how he help this nation and as far as the killing of Osama ben Laden I am very confident President Donald Trump would have been very determined to have taken care of such persons. Donald Trump as President has given me a more positive look that he cares about people and his country and that is what keeps him ahead of any other wannabe president. Do we really want to go back to the Obama era where things were not so good, we already had eight years of nothing and things that were questionable but were not? As I look at what is happening in the race for president, I hear many promises being made and a lot of those promises are scary because of what they are promising. Some of these promises are just plain absurd like this one free money but the question I ask is where is this money coming from? I'm also hearing of this nation becoming a socialist country this so-called socialist agenda has never worked just look at China, Russia, Cambodia, Cuba, North Korea and now the Venezuelans. Do you really want that to happen here in this nation that was so blessed by God? So, as the elections get nearer let's look at what happened in the 2016 elections at the time I was still in prison. As I saw Donald Trump win the election and how thought it was on liberals and the democratic party and how personal Hillary Clinton took the lost I prayed that she would get over the loss and just move on with her life and not be to depress that she would seclude herself from those who love her and want the very best for her. As time went on Hillary Clinton finally surfaces and when I saw the former Secretary of State her demeanor was not a happy one but looked like she was in a state of deep depression I kind of felt sorry for her at that time but I knew she would eventually recuperate from her state she was in. After a few weeks returning to the spotlight I was proven to be right Hillary Clinton wrote a book about the election and wrote about her thoughts and trying to explain to her constituents why she lost the election and her beliefs as to what went wrong. In her book she really puts the blame on everybody and not on herself. It was like she refused to take responsibility and I just thought, and she was running for President? That office must be taken with great responsibility and here she is blaming everybody but herself. What is wrong with this lady we win some and then we lose some but at the same time we must learn to take responsibility for our own actions whatever they may be good or bad. Its amazing people believe everything that was written in that book, well, at least her followers do; Well anyway it's out there in your local bookstores. Then we come to some of the most interesting people on our planet, which there are quite a few out there somewhere but here we have one who was in power but was fired by the President of the United States and its really strange to me about this man because he held the job of great responsibility it was a job of the most highest in Law Enforcement I thought these people in such position shouldn't have any bias towards who was president these people like those in the military had to respect the office of presidency regardless of their personal feelings.

CHAPTER FIVE

THE OFFICE THAT I am talking about is the Federal Bureau of Investigations doesn't the president have the power to appoint a director of his choice? and even the power to replace this post? The answer is under the constitution, yes. The democrats went ballistic when Comey the F.B.I. Director was fired and Comey himself, as the saying goes in prison started singing like a canary. The man was so upset and so were his top officials now listen closely these top officials who remained in the FBI colluded in private to see how they could get rid of the President of the Unites States Donald Trump. not all the Bureau was against President Trump my guess would be only the power hungry agents who were probably scared of the ax themselves were scrambling to find a way to get rid of the President now by getting together to plot a scenario to get rid of the president by any means necessary wouldn't that be called collusion? Well either way the problem I find with all of the things that were happening in Washington and with all the lies that came in about the Russian meddling in the elections, now all these things were actually already known by the democrats why did they not do anything about these crazy things back then or better yet why didn't President Obama do anything about what was already known during his administration? It seems to me the people who knew about these nefarious things should be held accountable and need to answer why nothing was done. These acts of omission are somewhat strange and do not make any sense at all when you really take a closer look at things. From what I understand as a nonpolitical person is that people at the top office of the FBI like McCabe, Rosenstein and several others. They must also look at Loretta Lynch what did she know? and why the secret meeting behind the bus with former President Clinton? Rosenstein is probably the one who came up with impeachment using the 25 amendment to the constitution or something like that, but under that amendment the president must be so ill that his sickness keeps him from performing the duties of the presidency or he must have mental Illness that again keeps him from performing his duties as President and non of those things were hindering President Donald Trump from performing his duty as president. This whole thing as I said started because Hillary Clinton lost the election. The office of the Federal Bureau of Investigation should never be involved in politics as they were in this election year this office is always to remain truthful, honest and with integrity they must never choose sides like they did. My belief in the integrity of the FBI has been tainted by certain questionable individuals who are still at work when they should all be in prison for perjury. but because it was against President Donald Trump it has been swept under the rug. I just hope and pray the FBI starts to build their integrity and get rid of those who are no good for the bureau. although some were so adamant about getting rid of President Trump, they made up these stories of Russian Collusion between President Trump and Russians and they know this was all and it still is false. When Comey was fired from his position as FBI director The two agents left in charge of the agency were McNab who was acting director after Comey got fired and the second in command who was also in a position of command was Rod Rosenstein the deputy director these two agents began to make up stories of collusion by President Trump and the Russian Government. It has been more than two years since this bogus investigation all started and even today as we wind up the second year of the investigation, that nothing has been found about the collusion theory and today as I hear more and more about this made up story it's just a waste of time but today after more than two years of B.S. They have added a new twist to it, it's called "obstruction" and even with that in place nothing seems to materialize, but yet the tax payers are putting up the money for these horrible accusations that really have no proof not one single proof! what has come out are indictments that have nothing to do with President Trump nor anything solid against him what I believe is the people who started all these accusations should be sent to prison for perjury against congress because they did actually lied to congress. The democrats are so inclined to believe such a lie time and again. Today as I write this I keep asking myself why is Rod Rosenstein still at the FBI when he himself cannot be trusted I saw him while he was being questioned by congress he had a mocking smirk on his face like he was getting the last laugh maybe he did because to me when I saw that smirk I just said to myself this man is making a fool out of congress and everyone else who are believing what he's ditching out. As I look more and more at the Mueller's Investigation I find a very disturbing thing going on and that is that some of the people who voluntarily chose to testify are being hauled off to prison for lying to congress but that's not all I'm finding a nexus and that is those who had any affiliation with President Trump before he was elected are being prosecuted for lying. What about all the others who don't have any affiliation with the President and there are many who testified in congress under oath and are not truthful. I'm talking about McCabe, Rosenstein, Or, the Lawyer and the FBI agent who was having an affair with a government attorney and who wanted to get something against the President why aren't they going to prison? What about the Judge who signed off on the warrant to entrap the President why are they still free? did they not also lie about their part in this egregious act of treason? It might not be treason in their book but in my book that's what I would call it. for this reason, the definition of the word treason according to (Dictionary Dot Com, is "The offense of betraying one's country especially by attempting to kill the sovereign or overthrow the government.") Some of these elected officials were even trying to us the United States constitution article II. This article deals with the Executive Branch to try and remove President Trump out of office. They must prove that the president is unable to perform his or her duties. The President can also be removed for crimes and misdemeanors. What crimes has President Donald Trump committed? have they even read article II of the Constitution? If they haven't read it, they need to read the article and understand what it was intended for. And then maybe they will see how wrong some of these leftists are in wanting to impeach President Donald Trump. As I had said the division of this country is being blamed on our President, but as I take a more

28   DELUSION CONFUSION COLLUSION

interest as to what the news media together with the haters of Donald Trump are all about I find that some of these stories were bogus and not the Presidents doing, take for instant the story about how the children were being housed, in one news cast they were showing children asleep on the floor wrapped in what looked like or was aluminum foil it was later discovered that this was during President Obama's term and this footage of the children on floors were used by the "fake news" to make people believe this was a current event. Why wasn't none of this reported back then? Obama separated children from their mothers long before President Trump came to office and the regular news media were ok with what Obama was doing at the time. I remember when Obama was campaigning for the Presidency; he was making a speech and I turned to my wife and said you see that guy he gives an eloquent speech but its all very deceiving. and I thought to myself he's either a demagogue or his speech is full of sophistry. My wife's a democrat and I'm a republican but we normally vote on issues and that day I told my wife I'm not voting for Obama because I can see through all that eloquent speech, he was making was very unsteady in my guts. We both voted for McCain God bless his soul. Of course, we all know what happened in that election. The majority took the bait hook line and sinker not only once but twice. When Donald Trump was elected President, he was right in what he said when he said, "I inherited a mess." Its not easy being the President of the most prosperous, powerful and blessed nation in the world. Many a president has made that fact known. this division has even infected the public those who for some reason or another want to see the president fail when President Donald Trump nominates someone for office the democrats and the liberals will go to any length to discredit those who the president nominates take one of the supreme court nomination of Brett Kavanaugh this poor man went to such length to prove his innocents and the democratic party refused to believe a word he said, it was so intense the FBI could not find any truth to what he was being accused of, but yet we have a democrat Cory Booker who also wanted to discredit his nomination this is where I found it to be ironic Cory Booker did not believe Kavanaugh and Booker had already convicted and sentence Kavanaugh in his mind. Booker should have said nothing because according to some news report Cory Booker himself has a black cloud hanging over his head and its a dozy not many people have heard it because it was not in the media long enough, but his own honesty and integrity are also in question. Its been reported that Cory Booker has been accused of groping a female individual some years back, whether true or not, why was it not investigated and given enough coverage as what Kavanaugh went through. Justice Kavanaugh I salute you sir for standing your ground and also being a member of the supreme court of the united states thank you for your service and the same salute goes out to all the supreme court justices. As for other news that I came across was how did a certain member of the Senate get this position? some reports coming out say this member slept her way to the top even the man she had an affair with has made it very clear that he did help her with her career and this man is none other than the former mayor of San Francisco Mr. Brown while he himself was married he admits to the affair. how come nobody wants to know about this Senators self respect which to me she has none. what about her honesty and ethics why did it not make news like the trump stories that make news? maybe because it happened twenty years ago or longer but when it comes to the Trump stories it makes front page and stays there for awhile. This same person whom the Senator had an affair with is also saying he helped Nancy Pelosi and senator Feinstein get to the top, now he did not mention how he helped them. He's just saying he helped them. Maybe the same public who wants to discredit President Trumps nominees maybe they should want to find out how Speaker Nancy Pelosi and Senator Feinstein were helped by this former San Francisco Mayor. While I was in state prison, I saw many foreigners who were waiting to be deported back to where they were from. I mean there were many whose only crime was being here illegally I asked myself why the state is holding on to these people for long periods of time I've seen some who were held for maybe two, three, or more years. I heard they do this for the state to make money off the federal government, well these things are in my other book called "The Twisted System" soon to be published.

Chapter Six

I have spoken with many who were in prison for illegally entering the country and many are here because they want a better life than what they have back home some want to come in legally but the wait time is to long and they need to get money home to feed their children, and many others were in prison not only for being here illegally but for drug crimes and many other variety of crimes. I am amazed at how the left has reacted to the immigration situation when the subject of securing the border with a barrier came up when I talk to these foreigners who were here illegally the majority of those I spoke to said if such thing is put in place their main concern was "How am I going to cross over again" and I'm talking about those who were in prison for drug crimes trafficking drugs is what they do for a living this is the only thing they know how to do, and they need to make a living and to be in the United States it's hard for them to work a decent job because not many business would hire an Illegal foreigner without proper papers so they do what they can to make money to send back home, so to them drugs are an easy choice for them. And then I also talked to those who were in prison for taking illegals to the north once they crossed the border and these were American prisoners awaiting transfer to a federal facility, they told me some of the reasons they did what they did. Some did it because of the economy at the time, others didn't like the pay they were getting at their regular jobs so this to them was a good way of increasing their income, then others just didn't want to work a regular job. Just imagine the fee for coming to the U.S. is 2,000-5,000 dollars per person so a lot of it was the money they could make. The democrats are doing their best to put the immigration problem on the President but from what I've seen and heard this problem has been going on for a long time now. The "fake news media" and many of these talk shows that come out late at night has made it to look like President Trump created this problem. Nothing can be further from the truth. We come now to the immigration problem it has been revealed that some of these former Presidents along with the approval of congress had a barrier in mind but nobody did anything about this endeavor why? few of the presidential candidates made promises about immigration but those promises were never kept. These same candidates also made promises about moving the U.S. Embassy from Tel Aviv to Jerusalem, but never did anything to make it become a reality. When Donald Trump was elected President, he kept his campaign promises and today he continues to make good on his promises. As I would do every morning while I was in prison I would turn the Fox and Friends news and the news would be going on about how the so called "Fake news" would not report the good president Trump was doing, but they did report all the bad stuff that was mostly not true. As I mention earlier in this book about the accusation about colluding with the Russians government so he could win the presidency this caused major divisions in this country. It brought me to the time when the government was cracking down on people who were suspected of being communist of course this happened before I was even born, but I had read about it and studied a little about what was happening and a lot of people were really not involve with communism at all, many were convicted or blacklisted for being a friend of a communist person I mean back then even if you just said hi! to a known communist the investigation into your life would begin and if word got out you were being investigated for being affiliated with a communist person that was it for you many entertainers and actors were being shun because they were on the governments list of people who were believed to be communists. These blacklisted people could not even find work. It was a horrible time in history. The democratic party and those who didn't want Trump to be president started to create a story of Trump secretly meeting with Russian agents to commit criminal acts so with the help of the FBI they decided this needed to be further investigated and so those in the democratic party and those in position to make decisions came up with a plan and that plan was to put a special counsel to investigate the newly elected president of the United States and see if they can come up with anything to remove him from office. The left as they are called have gone so far as to even investigate those who are friends of the president why is there so much animosity toward President Trump and his family what has he done to those who hate him? What I am talking about is those people who never even met the president personally why do they hate him and those who support his presidency? When President Trump lowered the taxes as he had promised many of his enemies were against such cuts, but if you take a closer look it has been the decision that has made a difference in the economy it has helped everyone including those who are against his presidency. As I try to make sense of these entertainers who are bent in keeping our nation divided and the hatred alive and well and I see what President Donald Trump has done so far. I am very proud to be a republican in support of Donald Trump because when I was little I remember a speech that was done by a very famous President and the words still ring in my ears since I first heard it and it was this very quote "Ask not what your country can do for you, but ask what you can do for your country" and if you really take a good look around you, you will come to the same conclusion as I have Donald Trump is doing for this country like Mr. John F. Kennedy quoted to this country many years before. As I said before what has Obama and the democratic liberals and those who oppose what Trump has done. The economy is in great shape, unemployment is at a record low, Jerusalem is now the capital of Israel, The stock market is in high gear, The North Korea is no longer a threat as long as open negotiations are held, look at NAFTA he's managed to make it where everyone involved is treated with fairness. President Trump has also manage to get out of the Iranian deal that to me was very egregious and not any good what were they thinking of when the Obama administration was making such a deal again this deal was more in the advantage of the Iranians than for anyone else's advantage. The Gross domestic product is doing a lot better under President Donald Trump than it has done with Obama being in charge. While in state prison some of the inmates who saw what was going on in the regular news couldn't understand if

President Donald Trump is doing good for the country why are they degrading him and treating him with contempt? I managed to talk to a few of these inmates and help them see what the truth is by comparing news reports. The hatred towards our President has begun to spill over to his supporters and it was the so called "Fake News" and those talk shows that were spreading nothing but negative information, on top of that so was the liberals and democrats they were all having a field day about the lies that Donald Trump was spreading when in reality it was the other way around. This hatred has made ordinary people hate each other for no apparent reason, So much so that some of Trumps administration workers were being harassed while having dinner with their families and friends and all this was being supported by some of the democratic political party like Maxine Waters, Cory Booker and Eric Holder these are the ones who were actually caught on camera promoting violence as a means to intimidate those who are supporters of President Donald J. Trump. they should have been arrested for instigating a fight or riot why is Maxine and Booker still in office after approving what I would call violence toward Trump supporters isn't that prejudice, Hatred, and profiling. neither the right wing nor the left wing are our enemies, but the left wing has made it out to be that way this is a good way of causing division amongst ourselves we all have a right to chose who we support and this should never be the cause for violence. The people who hold office should lead by example not by violence. I was really surprised what Eric Holder as suggesting when he was caught on tape and this person was the highest law enforcement officer of the United States where did he get educated? or better yet what was he taught in Law School and college? What

I think about now when I reflect on these elected officials and appointed officials and their demeanor all I can say is they deceived the public by putting on a different face in office. Put these people in normal setting out comes their true colors. I wonder do they have any scruples or dignity for themselves? The success of Donald Trump is making many haters more agitated because they don't want to see him succeed neither does the media nor those talk shows they are not reporting the truth what they do report is a twisted truth which is also causing hatred and division amongst our own citizens. Maybe those people would like nothing more than to see bloodshed and chaos amongst our own country man It seems to me they don't like Unity and harmony but rather hatred and evil at least that's what I have observed all this time I hope I'm wrong but its really hard to think other wise. Especially when the same people who were voted into office condone such behavior. It's funny how many liberals and democrats have made the wearing of a simple red hat with the words "Make America Great Again" so abhorrent and to signify racial slurs when all we want is to make America mean greatness for all people of all races who are considered Americans by birth or by naturalization let me just say this to those who think a simple hat is racial and discriminatory I am a Mexican American born in the USA My parents were from Mexico well my dad was and he became a US citizen many years ago and I would like to tell all those haters I wear my hat proudly and I have nothing against anyone or anybody I just see one race and that's the human race Glory be to God almighty in Jesus Name. we are all human beings If you really hate a simple hat for what it stands for then you should really look in the mirror and see what you see. Just like me when I look at myself in the mirror I see a good man living in a great country where I can prosper and live as I please as long as I am not breaking any laws or causing trouble for myself I live in the United States of America under the protection of the almighty God for I still believe in One Nation Under God. With a President who wants the very best for the people, and I do mean all people. Just remember John F. Kennedy's quote let me remind you if you forgot it "Ask not what your country can do for you, but what you can do for your country," What I would like to ask those liberals and democrats what exactly do they stand for and what is it that they are looking to accomplish?

Chapter Seven

As I look at the news it seems to me their looking to make themselves look good when in reality they are only making things worst as the days go by. My belief currently is that many democrats and liberals are out to destroy this nation with what they want to accomplish. Those on the left have a very warped sense of thinking and the regular news media seems to fuel their Ideology by reporting what is to me nothing more than lies and heresies this type of reporting only fuels the left and makes them believe it's ok to do what they do. The truth is Donald Trump has done more for this country in two years than any other President in my lifetime including President Ronald Reagan and President Reagan was a good President in that time and era. I hear about how the hard left say "President Obama Started the economic recovery", if that was so why didn't Hillary Clinton win the election she was only going to follow what President Obama had done for this country by keeping in place all he had done, but not only that, she was going to raise taxes another 15% I think the public saw that and they just decided enough was enough what we need is someone who is not a politician and that's where Donald Trump came in he was not a politician but a shrewd business man and a self made billionaire at that. As I had said before what did Obama do for this nation absolutely nothing but weakened our economic system by putting in place all those regulations that made it hard for the business sector to do their job which kept unemployment at a ridiculous rate. Let me just give you what was happening in 2015 before the election. Unemployment rate was at 5.3% and that's what was reported because many were not counted because they stopped looking for work and the GDP was not doing so well either just look at the numbers for the year 2015 First Quarter 3.3% second Quarter 3.3% third Quarter 1.0% and in the fourth Quarter it was at 0.4% It was going down not up. So where do these people get that Obama was the maker of our now prosperous economy every person in the United States has been having more money in their pockets than it was in the two terms President Obama served, but lets give him credit he did put more money in the pockets of the Iranian regime when he gave them pallets of cash for no apparent reason or at least I have not heard one. And so, this country continues to hate a President who has made more progress in his promises than any other president. People come on what's wrong with us are we really that blind to see who is really looking after our own good. They have time and again tried to make Donald Trump a person who is not fit to be president. They have made up stories about his life and dealings the news never reports anything that Trump does is good the news would much rather report one what is not good than what is good. As the months and years pass by, we the people must take a real close look at what our future holds. We must ask ourselves a really sobering question are we better off today than we were when Obama was President? but we must ask that question and look around us and see how far President Trump has taken us and if you think for one minute that our president is dividing us you must really be mentally blind in my book. Open your mind and see the roses and smell the coffee Wake-Up!!! or we'll end up in a place we soon regret making, lets take for instance the mid-term elections the public has given control of the House to the democrats and Liberals it's been an up hill battle for President Trump to secure our borders and keep our citizens safe. When the democrats took the house one of the worst things that came out of such win is there was a power hungry individual by the name of Nancy Pelosi this woman was so hungry to be the speaker of the house and her intentions were already on her mind and let me just say this in my honest opinion she cares nothing for this country or the citizens of this country had she cared about the American people there would have been a wall on our borders. Some homeowners have made it a priority to put fences or walls along our properties pe-rimeters' to protect what belongs to us. We build neighborhoods and surround it with security gates and walls and only those who live there can enter and keep the rest out of our neighborhoods we call them Colonies we also have Apartment complexes with gated entrance that only those who live in the complex can enter and the way to enter is through codes some living communities have their own police security if anyone is caught in the property illegally they are either arrested or thrown off the property. People live in these places because they are secure and makes them feel safe, but yet we have those who live in these places and are against securing our borders and be secure in our persons I call those peo-ple hypocrites and fakes doing the opposite of what they believe in.

Now let's be realistic here, how many of you who oppose the securing of our border would leave your doors wide open while you sleep at night and let your children sleep with the windows open with no fence on your yard to secure the premises?. I think we all agree we must have some kind of security for the sake of our children and grandchildren. I think even Nancy would agree on this but yet when it comes to the Citizens of our lovely country Pelosi is against any border wall this is what makes me believe she has no interest in protecting anyone but herself and this would be very selfish. What Nancy Pelosi is standing for is only hurting our country it makes our safety questionable. Are we safe with Nancy Pelosi as leader? I think not we must vote her out of office we need better leaders who will look after our nation and its people every senator and every congressman took an oath of office and that is to protect and defend the constitution of the United States I don't think she's living up to her oath, I mean this makes her look like an advocate to destroy this country's sovereignty. It is my belief in hearing what Nancy Pelosi has to say is not of any use or helps in anyway what I see is a person who is very self centered, pompous and prideful she has an agenda and that agenda is only about her, and the power this country has given her I don't think she has any intentions of looking for the good of the people only what makes her more powerful and to me that is a very dangerous position to be in. In prison there's always a power struggle on who would be leader or who would run the living quarters in prison it was never a safe place to be. Another Representative who to me kind of looks like the cartoon about the bull dog and the little dog always following this bull dog around its kind of funny and the reason it reminds me of these characters is because every time Nancy Pelosi has something to say the man is always around her like a shadow and makes a statement about what Nancy had said it's kind of like he needs to be around her or he's lost. This individual I'm talking about is non other than Schumer himself this man is another one who could care less about his country and basically has nothing good to say about anything to me he is like Nancy Pelosi's shadow they both need to be voted out as soon as possible. I wish no harm to either of them I just don't think they are good in the office they both hold. What this country needs are more people who will look after his neighbor than to try and destroy that which God has blessed so Dearly which is this country. We must unite together and be as one not divided like we are today if you don't like the President it's ok just don't create a division in this country the bible say that God is the one who appoints our Presidents and our leaders we must therefore unite and make this a great nation the way God intended it to be when we cast our vote ask God to direct you on whom you should vote for. We are coming close to the end of this presidential term but yet we hear of another senator who wants to start another investigation on our President has he not learned that after two years of investigating President Trump for collusion or obstruction they have yet to find anything to me this has been all a waste of tax payers money and we could do better things with our money than to waste it foolishly on nothing that is not of value to this country let us spend the money where it is really needed the most. As I said we are nearing that time of year where we are going to the poles again and elect our leaders again it has been planted in my heart to write to you these things that for some make no sense at all and for others its more confusing. I used to be in that confusing category of people I just voted the way I did because my parents voted that way so I never really listen to their speeches nor for what they stood for in those days. I thought all politicians were liars and crooks but as I grew in knowledge and understanding I found out I was voting for the wrong people you see I've been a born again Christian since I was 12 years of age. I educated myself and learned many things through reading and listening to other people and to listen with an opened mind. I studied the word of God intensely. I went to many classes where the word of God was taught and my understanding of the word grew and His word became more important to me and how I looked at life although I did not follow Gods word to a T I did have a very rough upbringing. What I have seen and experienced in life is maybe good for another book but today I want to focus on what is happening today in this country and maybe shed a little light where it needs to be shed I need to remind all who read this book I'm not perfect, but I am forgiven by the blood of Jesus Christ. So why is there so much hate for our elected President Donald Trump? I still wrestle with that question even today as I try to make sense of all this mess the democrats are creating. There are many in the left who have entered to run for President of the United States and many of these candidates are running to try to make this country a socialist country these candidates are also wanting to get rid of our border security those enforcement officers who are in charge of keeping drugs and illegal foreigners from entering our country without permission some have also come up with this platform of ridiculous promises that will be in my opinion very hard to swallow. I mean let me just say that these ideals are not going to go well with the community if they understand what is going to cost the american people. Here is a list of what they proposed to put in place once they are elected to office, what you'll realize is what they really plan to do is destroy this country and everything we stand for please you must realize that what is coming in the future for our blessed nation is nothing more than chaos and violence if the democrats get there way and what I've been hearing is they are so fired up to getting there agenda approved by the citizen of our country so they can have the power they are looking to gain for themselves, I don't think they care what happens to this country or the citizens of this country what they are proposing is having open borders eliminating the border patrols and those who are sworn to serve and protect this country and not only that they have a new platform and this is what they call it "The New Green Deal" well just read what this deal consist of

1. They want to up grade all buildings I still haven't heard what buildings all I heard was all buildings in this country.

2. To have Jobs for every American who can work. I know what your thinking your saying to yourself well that's not too bad, but just wait, it will surprise you when you see the rest of the list.

3. They want to get rid of all affordable energy.

4. Eliminate all air travel completely.

5. Eliminate all Nuclear Energy.

6. Eliminate 99% of all cars.

7. Free Education for everyone for life.

8. A Salubrious diet for all.

9. A House

10. Free Money for those not working or something to that effects

11. Ban Meat Completely from this country. (WOW! No more Fillet Mignon for Me.)

Now, is this what were aiming for? do you think this is good for our country.

CHAPTER EIGHT

LOOK WHAT JUST happened in New York City one of the biggest corporation has decided to scrub the deal of building their Second Head Quarters in that city and this is what Alexandria Ocasio-Cortez has just accomplished and she is gloating that her and her followers were able to stop a major corporation from coming to New York City and now her own party is very upset at her for what she has done oh, even the governor of New York is upset at what has just happened now let me just say is this something that an economics major would want to gloat over? and further more is what she did to Amazon a prelude of what to be expected for the future of the United States when it comes to International Relations which is also one of her major studies while at Boston University. If it is, we are in for a disaster and much more. All I can say is when the time comes that Ms. Ocasio is up for re-election please you must and I do mean must not even cast a single vote in her favor. what she did to amazon was the stupidest thing and this is what puts me at a quandary about Alexandria Ocasio -Cortez International Relations and Economic Studies. What I find hard to believe is this; she did to her own state where she was elected for congress and this is how she pays them back? she has single handedly cost that city billions of lost revenue for the city not to mention what it could have done to the job market in New York City all this in one day 25,000 high paying salaries up in smoke thanks to Alexandria Ocasio-Cortez New York's newly elected congresswoman. (Bravo!! lets give her a standing ovation there is more stupidity to come) many of us don't think this is what should be happening, but our Democrats are pushing this Platform and they are running with it. Personally, I think it's the stupidest Platform I myself have ever heard. First of all, let's take the refurbishing of all buildings in America this would be a massive undertaking if we decide to do this but there is a problem how would the workers get to work if we eliminate car travel? then the other question would be who is going to work this job if your giving away free money to those who refuse to work? and maybe say to themselves why work? I have a House I have Money coming in who needs to work?

So, we come to eliminating air travel how will we visit our love ones who have moved thousands of miles away? We can't fly our way there nor can we hop in a car and visit because we won't have one to travel in. I mean we might have the money but who will take us there? ridiculous right? Let us take a little scenario if I may and tell you about a hypothetical story. Two men were sitting outside one of the men's free home when one of them said something that insulted the other they both get into an altercation and during that altercation one stabs the other several times, how are the police force going to handle this or is there going to be any law and order with the so called "Green Deal" the badly stab man has no remedy but to die of his wound for lack of air travel or ambulance because all these thing's have been eliminated. Now that is nothing more than plain stupidity. I could give more stories and tell you why this "Green Deal" will not work and I can't believe how many dense people buy into this agenda.

I come to the Education side this I find many democrats are lacking and they should be the first to sign-up for this because I don't think they have a clue of what they are going to create.

What's with the elimination of meat if we eliminate beef the first thing that comes to my mind would be the massive amount of people who would be out of work and not able to find jobs, Oh but wait they are going to get free money (From where is this money suppose to come from?) We have just created a horrible economy that is stagnate or better yet nonexistence. The United States as we know it would be in a downward spiral that there would be no turning back and some of these left winged politicians actually believe it's a dream come true, No it's not a dream come true it's nothing but a horrible nightmare that we would never wake up from such a nightmare. What are these democrats thinking about I think they are out to destroy this country, or they lack the education of other countries who have made the mistake if wanting to be a socialist regime? We have Alexandria Ocasio Cortez Leading the march toward the destruction of this country or it could be she knows what would happen and so maybe for her it would be good because she can become the first woman in the United States to make her the "Dictator" Just as Castro became the dictator of Cuba. Now that's clever of her. What I see is she has started her own followers on the way to dooms day. Did New York make a mistake in voting for Alexandria Ocasio Cortez? They say Ocasio attended college and majored in "International Relations" and "Economics" I have a problem believing she finished her majors or even really studied such difficult courses. What strikes me so odd is why did she not wanted to debate her opponents when she was a candidate could it be that her lack or the understanding of what she was getting into was to much that she did not want the public to see how dense she really is. This brings me back to my prison days and what I came across, well this happened more than once. One day I was laying on my bunk when this inmate asked me if I would help him get paper work done so he could be transferred back to the county he was from and of course I told him I would help him and as I was finishing up his paper work I asked if he could read what I had written he said that he could not read or write; but that wasn't what bothered me about this man it was the fact that on his record they had him as a high School graduate and he even had his High School Diploma to prove his high school education I said "How can you not know how to read of write if you graduated from high school and you have proof that you finished high school." and he said "what happen was they were just passing me along because they did not want to bother with me." This is what bothered me, that the school faculty can just pass someone just because they didn't want to bother with him, I mean these inmates were somewhat smart in a sense, but they lacked the reading and writing skills. To me maybe that's what might have happened to Alexandria Ocasio Cortez. Now I'm saying reached her goal in a different way like Kamala Harris who from what I read probably made her way to the top that way, now I'm not saying Alexandria Ocasio-Cortez did the same I really don't know but it does make me think after so much talk from Ocasio-Cortez If we look at what is happening her affair with a married man was exposed by the lover himself, If we look at what is happening in our political arena we must wonder are these democrats looking after the safety of this country or is this a ploy to get elected? Alexandria Ocasio-Cortez also studied economics and boy we must wonder is this true? When you hear her talk about the so called green deal any economics major would certainly say "she's out of her mind" how is all this suppose to work? In my humble opinion I don't think she has a clue of what she is talking about because if she had really studied economics her agenda would not be the one she is pushing on us. The United State is full of very smart individual and they know this so called "Green Deal" is not going to fly. then we must look at our current President Donald Trump is he really looking out to keep America safe and prosperous? and the definitive answer is yes what he has done is make our nation the leader in the International Community that's more than I can say about the democrats who have now placed their names on the ballot for President. We look at each individual and assess what does that person stand for or what is this person about? Does this person really stand for the values of America and its citizen? As I have already mention we have spent so much money on an investigation that is full of nonsense and yet we are today looking at hiring another special counsel or something like that to keep or continue the so called colluding or obstruction investigation come on people give if a rest if nothing was found since 2016 then there is nothing to investigate why waste the money. Time and time again the democrats and the media don't want the President to be successful in his tenure as President, but I do have to say to all the democrats and Liberals and the "Fake Media" President Donald Trump has already succeeded. His success has benefited every American and every entity in the United States and yet we want to treat our President with disdain and contempt shame on you. Would you much rather this country be destroyed by those who are ignorant and have a stupid agenda on what direction this God blessed Nation should go? Did any of the candidates who have placed their names for president ever studied History? History is suppose to teach us our past mistakes we've made and what other countries have made. When we refuse to look at history how can we look at our future? and this list keeps growing when I see the list of those democrats who are running for the office of Presidency what I find is that none of those names is fit to be president not one not even Former Vice President Biden my opinion on this is because why didn't he questioned Obama when Obama released those known dangerous terrorist from Guantanamo Bay Cuba? or the time when again Obama gave pallets of cash American money to those Iranians who would be happy to blow up Americans in a heart beat why? I really Wouldn't want an Obama marionette taking office he might just call Obama for advice. and ruin the progress President Donald Trump has made with the economy, the trade deal with China, the denuclearization of the Korean Peninsula and many other great and wonderful things that Donald Trump has done and are yet to come. What the Democrats have done is made a mess of what should have been a smooth transition and they have managed to separate our nation against each other we must see them for who they really are. What is also happening is that the democrats want to keep the American people under slavery conditions just look at what they are offering there is nothing there that makes the individual a success all they are trying to do is hook the people with that proverbial carrot and make you think its what helps an individuals life, well as I see it the real reason is when the states or the Federal Government gives you something it comes with a hidden price take for instance free education or lets say college for the sake of argument once you have excepted that offer you are now a slave to the one whom you took the offer from and they would make sure you know they paid it for you so was it really free not a chance you owe the government for the education they paid for you, and the pay back will come right after you graduate. It could be in any form they want because after all, you owe them, is this freedom? I think not. I say this because I am reminded about what the Bible says "a borrower becomes the lenders slave." You will not be at liberty to do what you want you'll have to answer to the government take all these government programs we have in place Lease Housing, Snap or (Food Stamps) and other programs the government has for every little thing you want to do on your own you must report it to the government or be out of the program these programs were establish to help the individual who has fallen into hard times a way to get back on there feet but it is not so because many are trapped in this cycle because when they do get a job and start getting a little bit back on there feet the government takes away what it gave you or wants its money back no matter how many years you worked hard and paid your taxes they want it back or they'll take it by tagging your wages and then guess what your back to square one depending on the government. To me that's slavery. what President Donald Trump is doing is giving back your dignity and self respect and if we don't see that which is so obvious then we must be blind. President Donald Trump has kept his promises and continues to look after the American people whether born or became citizens its all the same to him.

CHAPTER NINE

I FIND IT so disturbing that the democrats do not play a fair game when it comes to politics we must all look back at what happened during the Kavanaugh confirmation this man was accused of sexual violation during his college years and the democrats had already convicted and ready to sentence this man and these were just allegations it just so happened that these accusation were also investigated and it seem like the accuser was not able to remember key issues and during the FBI investigation they also had doubt if anything really happened but the democratic party would not leave it alone they dragged this man and his wife through the ringer and made a spectacle of Mr. Kavanaugh and his family its been some time since these atrocities occurred and today as I write these pages there are allegations that have come before the Senate and Republicans what I am talking about is what is going on in the State of Virginia elected Governor of Virginia and the Attorney General are both accused of being racist and on top that the now Lieutenant Governor of Virginia is being accused of sexual assault and the victim is even talking about these accusations why isn't the democratic party issuing an investigation of these three people and where is the so called "me too movement?" There are several issues at hand today that concerns me when it comes to the Democratic Party and Liberals why don't they answer question regarding all these allegations we even have an allegation of sexual assault on Cory Booker where has that issue gone did the democrats sweep this under the carpet It doesn't matter whether its a homosexual act or heterosexual a sexual assault is a very serious charge. Then we have allegations of Adultery by a female senator who continues to decieve the public when she said she used marijuana in her college years while listening to Tupac and some other artist She graduated from law school she graduated from law school in 1989 and according to the investigation that was done to see if this was truth they found out this marijuana story is faux because these musical entertainers were not even on the scene. Now the smoking could be true, but the other half of that story is false story my best bet is Kamala Harris wants to impress the liberals of California that's all I can figure out after looking at the short clip of the talk show she appeared on. We then have Pocahontas well That's what President Donald Trump calls her she has made her self to be equal to native Indians and after a DNA test this was just a hog wash and what has been reported was she might have done this to get special treatment of special privileges by claiming native American status. There are more ridiculous things, but I think you get the point are we to put our trust on such people?

We must keep our ears and eyes open and see what and where is this nation headed if the democrats take control. because democracy as we know it will be a thing of the past in this country I urge all Americans whether you're a liberal, Democrat, Republican, or an Independent we must never let this nation fall in the hands of the socialist or we will all be regretting it later if not sooner. If the democrats get their way with doing what they want to do and that is to raise the taxes on every body especially the wealthy this nation in no time will become a copy of a third world country. Socialism has never worked and it will never work Alexandria Ocasio-Cortez should follow my recommendation and read up on the following dictators and how they came into power. if not at least read what has been happening in their country or has already happen here is the list.

1. (Mengistu Haile Meriam) 1977-1991 He was influence by Marxist Leninist Policies

2. (Zidane Rahman) Bangladeshi Politician and was the First Military Dictator.

3. (Then She) Leader of Burma when Monks protested his leadership, he had them beaten severely that some died as the result of these beatings.

4. (Islam Karamu) 1989-1991

5. (Hu Jintao) 6th President of the People's Republic of China 2003

6. (King Swati III) King of Swaziland here people lived on less than one dollar a day.

7. (Fidel Castro) Cuba's dictator

Today there are few socialist Countries and this is the list according to Wiki

1. The Republic of China
2. Cuba
3. Laos
4. Socialist Republic of Vietnam

What we need to do is study these countries and really know what Socialism all is about. I Recommend that Alexandria Ocasio-Cortez take some courses on Foreign Studies with emphasis on socialism and its effects.

There are many more but just read a little bit of these dictators' life and how they ruled and just what or how they got the position of dictator or Ruler. I made this list because it is my belief Ms. Ocasio-Cortez has no clue of what she is standing on as far as her Ideology to me she's like those inmates I met in prison they were smart but because they couldn't read or write they made look as if they knew what they were talking about but in reality they knew nothing at all when it came to Math, History or anything else. These people I believe are called walking Illiterates. when I see Alexandria Ocasio-Cortez and what she stands for and when she was asked for a debate and she refused it kind of reminded me of an incident I went through and this is how it all happened I was in town in this city and I remember there would be a convention for cardiologists and at the time my business was doing good but I was in the process of opening a billing service so I needed to come up with something where I could meet doctor and give my business cards away so when I remembered about this convention for cardiologist I went to this convention and pretended to be a cardiologist because only cardiologist were allowed at this convention well being in the Medical Supply Business you come across many doctors of different specialties I knew the lingo and so I managed to get into this conference of doctors pretending to be a cardiologist and so as I look at Alexandria Ocasio-Cortez could she be a Hoax and really no nothing about what she stands for I mean why would you avoid to answer certain question of explain how this green deal is suppose to work? I might be wrong or maybe not, and I hope I am wrong and she's not a Hoax but from what I've been through in life its hard not to think of these things. Today as we come closer to the 2020 elections many of the democratic party are going to put their names on the ballot for president. This will be a flooded card as I listen to the issues at hand and what each candidate stands for, I am again filled with so much information that really is just plain stupid and not at all what would help this country stands for. I heard former Vice President Biden who was speaking in Germany and his speech was nothing more than a put down of this nation he told everyone in attendance who was at hearing distance that the United States was an Embarrassment now this man held the second highest office of the United States and speaks about the United States with disdain and contempt and I wonder what kind of President would he make? The thought just makes me sick. As I look back at what I can remember about previous Presidents it's that those who love their country were always the best Presidents to hold office now you may not see it that way, but I do. I look at what is already on the ticket and I see nothing more than self serving candidates who seem to want to destroy America as we know it today. To me the only true Patriot who has looked after America is our present President Donald Trump and Vice President Mike Pence. I will vote for them this time around because the first time Trump was running for president I was in prison and did not get a chance to vote. I hope and pray God will hear my prayers and touch the hearts of the many of those individuals who have hate in their hearts and that would soften their hearts and see that as Americans we need Donald Trump to finish what he has started and that God would surround our President and Vice President with angels of protection in Jesus name.

CHAPTER TEN

WHAT HAS HAPPENING to our country is we are having to listen to lies and false accusation we have been deceived in believing that those on the left are for making America a place to live and enjoy life but it was not so, the lie became more powerful and more believable. Well its time to open our eyes to the truth. Stop being led by the pied piper, because if you don't this country will be led to an Economic and Political Slaughter just look at the example of Venezuela. When Hugo Chavez was campaigning for the leadership of Venezuela he made promises to the people and blamed all its troubles and headaches on the capitalist and he promise the people relief by becoming a socialist nation and told the people that they would share in the wealth once the government takes control of private enterprise sectors and the people believed all his lies even the entertainment sector were endorsing his candidacy just like here in the United States. The same thing is being done here just as it was done in Venezuela. After the elections the country became a socialist country and many of their wealthy people fled the country and then the worst happened Venezuela ran out of money and wealth the president that is now in place "Maduro" is a carbon copy of Hugo Chavez because he was a follower of Hugo Chavez and well now they are in dire straits and this happened because the people of Venezuela believed in a great lie, are we going to be dense enough to believe a lie from these democratic socialist who want to make Gods country a socialist nation? there are no jobs, food, water, sometimes they can't even afford toilet paper or just the basic necessities. Now I ask you; America is this what you really want? While I was living in Florida, I met a few Venezuelans, and these people whom I met were very friendly people. I am deeply move with sadness with what I see in the news about the calamity that has hit Venezuela we should try and help them as much as we are able too, we must reach out to them with humanitarian aide. As I have mention before not every politician is interested in the problems of the American people. they're out for themselves. Let's look at what was going on before Donald Trump came on to the scene. There was a time when these same politicians that were in office when Obama was President were trying to figure out how to deal with the immigration problem, This immigration problem has been a problem for the United States since long before Donald Trump was even thinking about the presidency but still this problem needed a solution, but the solution was short in coming President Donald Trump has made several attempts in trying to solve this problem but Pelosi and Schumer would not even hear what he or the secretary of homeland security had to say. Now is this what grown ups do shut themselves up and behave worst than children? I mean Schumer said the president threw a tantrum, but what I saw was a hateful man who cares nothing for this country or the people had they cared they would have listen to what both, Trump and the Secretary of homeland security had to say. but instead left the room without a compromise there was a time President Trump said he was willing to give passage to those in the DACA program, so they would have their chance at becoming U.S. citizens, and again Pelosi and Schumer ignored his request. Now what I understood is President Donald Trump wanted to give passage to a lot more than just the 800,000 we're talking about. it was more than a million who were already in this country. Pelosi and Schumer brilliantly made people believe that the President is at fault here, but, as I see it, it is Pelosi and Schumer who refused what the President had to offer it's in my opinion that those two are playing the part of dividers of this country, Now lets really look at what and who is behind all these things and you will see things just like I do, that Nancy Pelosi and Chuck Schumer are not really that concerned about wanting to do anything about immigration, this all has to with President Donald Trump they can not stand Trump as being able to succeed. What they want more than anything else is for Donald Trump to be a failure. If we look at footage of when President Barrack Obama was in office they had an agreement and were willing to spend lots of money on the border to secure it with a barrier, so after so many discussions and no end in sight they all agreed and came up with a border barrier but nothing was ever done about it, and if they did do something about it this was not enough. Just like the embassy of Irreal many candidates made a promise to move the U.S. Embassy to Jerusalem, but nobody did anything close to it they all "forgot" the Issue. The accomplishment President Donald Trump has been successful in has benefited everyone democrats, Liberals, Independents and Republicans alike it has no respecter of color, sexual orientation or religious affiliation. The left has also been so vulgar in their speech and some have made it very clear that they have been aiming at taking a violent stand on those who support President Donald Trump why would this even happen Maxine Waters is a very outspoken person when it comes to violence her speeches are aimed at taking a violent stand, now, is this what America is all about? If not, then what we need to do is speak our voice and not re-elect such a person. Violence has never been the answer to our problems, and we must make that clear to Maxine Waters and all of those who think like her once and for all. When our leaders' resort to violence then what we get is heart aches and pain and sorrow. I for one am not a violent person but I will defend myself against any bodily harm that might be coming towards me. we now look at news media that has gone and joined the left. When I was going to school we were taught that the news media never played only one sided news reporting and I really thought this to be true but what I have seen lately is very disturbing the news has made if a habit if being so bias and not reporting what is the truth, it has taken it upon themselves to report a lopsided news cast and what has happened there too is what has also divided the nation the news can be very influential and at times can be very damaging and it can start a big wild fire when the news decides it will report only what they see fit to them, whether its truth or twisted truth why has the news media become so hateful of our elected President Donald Trump? This kind of loathing brings nothing more than violence towards our own country men and women and believe it or not it infiltrates our families. I for one stopped looking at ABC it used to be my favorite news cast until I started to notice that it was reporting unreliable news, and this just took me by surprise. I still think that deep down inside these news casters really do know deep down in their hearts That Donald Trump is doing a fantastic job as president, but for some reason they feel it's better to be a demagogue than to lose their position of anchor. just like those politicians who are nothing more than demagogues themselves just so they can be in a position of power. The years since Donald Trump became President, they have been very good productive times because of the Economic upturn. What we really need is more candidates like President Donald Trump those who have a back bone and are not afraid to do what is best for its people and the country those who have character and Integrity and who will stand for America and not be embarrassed by her this is what we need and we need this because as you all have seen President Donald Trump has achieved this great venture he promised and he delivered. Now who is going to fill those shoes when his second term is over? We should be happy and celebrating in the streets. There are Hundreds of thousands of people who want of come to this country why? Because once again this nation is a prosperous and strong nation many want to Identify themselves with greatness and guess what America this is a great nation once again why would anybody want to change its demeanor sure we have our problems but it is those who care about this nation who will always step up to the plate and do their very best to make America safe and secure and to have self respect for themselves not degrading and disrespecting our great nation. Like what Joe Biden did in Germany that was just awful of an American citizen to do can you Imagine just how these leaders must have looked at Joe Biden when he said what he said? In my opinion be gave America a black eye. We see and hear all these things that are being said and done by the left and not one word about the bad things being said about our nation, We have sexual allegations and Adulterous behavior and we tend to say or do nothing and this is from those same people or group of people who are ready to lynch and behead some one who has not even been given a fair hearing or chance to defend themselves are we really that ignorant. I don't think so I think we are so used to hearing a lie that we have forgotten what it feels like to hear the truth and we are so complacent that we expect that behavior from our politicians and so it's just a normal thing. We must not ever get so used to those behavior that we lose our own self-respect I have more respect for truth than fake or false pretentious people. What all this proves is we have a bunch of power-hungry idiots who want to do nothing more than to destroy our culture and way of life. I love my country I was born in and I will defend it to the death I don't like to carp so I do what I can do and accomplish what I feel is good for me. I hear many people complain about how the rich are getting richer and the poor are getting poorer and I will tell you this kind of thinking doesn't do you any good, all it does is make you angry and well it also makes one not want to do anything at all for themselves. After all these years of hearing all these people spew out what they thought of the well to do I was surprise to hear and learned that John F. Kennedy mother make this statement. I guess she was making a speech or something but what she said made real good sense and I will always carry this in my heart until I die and it took for me to go to prison to learn this and this is what she said "Just because you were born poor doesn't mean you have to stay there". I mean I heard that, and it really hit home and I thought to myself and this is the only country where you can be that successful. This you won't find it any other third world country not even in a socialist regime. I have looked at who ever is in office will determine how fast or how slow my success would be and this is how I see it if the President whom we elected or those in the congressional and senate are stubborn and only want to slow things down and make the economy move at a slow pace then it will definitely be more hard work to reach my goal but if we elect those in office who are looking for the betterment of the people then my goals of economic success would be more reachable and less time consuming than the first scenario. So, what is it going to take for your success to be certain the elected officials must be on your side and only want what is best for you. Never settle for anything less than this. We must also recognize we have to do our part if we ever want to be a success. If we take what has just happen to Venezuela they are in a state of complete chaos The President of that country made a statement to the people during his campaign that Venezuela will not be a capitalist country and if that were to happen he would arm himself and defend that country against capitalist. Let us understand one thing about Venezuela President Maduro is and will be Venezuela's new dictator and there is nothing anyone can do unless there is some sort of Intervention. As I look at what is going on in this South American country, I think of what our Democrats, Liberals and Democratic Socialists who want to change this system of Government that has made this country what it is today. What they are promising is just not feasible and maybe if I can make some sense of what is in store for what they are promising this is what I believe will happen if we allow the left to have their way; Lets start with work for every body to me it will be something like force labor, you will work where the government has placed you to work, and you will receive an allowance for doing your work. Then lets look at free housing how is this suppose to happen well the only way this could happen is if the government takes control of all apartments and houses lets say a person owns more than one house then that person has to give up all properties except only one for the owner if that person happens to own apartment complexes or condos and things like that well. it will become the government properties how else will people get to live in homes for everyone. Now let's look at health care for everybody I have not heard any politician say that this health care for everyone is and will be including those with existing illnesses. Well any way my only thought about those people with such illnesses would be that if these existing conditions are terminal then my opinion on this would be to just let you die in peace and not bother with trying to help with your malady because it will be costly and a burden some to the state so it would be much easier and less costly to just put you to sleep like we do a very severely sick animal or maybe your costing the government to much trouble and even your age might be a factor after all they have this bill out there where its ok to get an abortion when the living baby is out of the womb just figure it this way your in late senior years why should the government bother in keeping you alive? They need the money to send people to college free. Then let's look at free college for everyone is it really going to be free? It's my belief this will come as a price to the college student. something like this; the government paid your college now you owe them and you will pay one way or another maybe by working where they believe you will be of great use with no compensation because you are already receiving free money I mean I don't know from where this money will come from but that's what I believe will happen. What I have just given you are scenarios of what I believe will happen just look at those countries I have listed earlier look at how these people are treated and taken care of, if we allow those Liberals, Democrats and Democratic Socialists take control of this beautiful nation is this what we really want for ourselves and our families? Oh, by the way this all will happen gradually and like the fore mention countries we too will be in chaos and turmoil. Many Nations will look at us and will ridicule us and treat us with disdain and scorn. and for all you journalist who reported nothing but fake news your days will be numbered too. What I mean is you will only report what the ruler will allow you to report. The so called news will be censored by the government, and many journalist and news casters will be out of work but don't fret you'll also have free money and a house to live in if you manage to stay out of prison for reporting what you should not have reported thanks to the government you sided with so much in your freedom days. and you'll remember at times when you were going against a President who wanted nothing but the very best for this country, but that was not good enough right? The judicial system as we know it today will be full of corruption. In those days we will be nothing more than slaves just as what we had before and What a living hell, we will be in. My real concern at this time is for those I will leave behind like my children and grand children who are the future of this country what are we doing to them. When I hear People say President Donald Trump is a liar I think of the regular news media those that twist the real story around to bring hate against some one who has made this nation a lot better than it was four years ago and still wants to accomplish more things for this nation. I see Donald Trump is not after power he's after the betterment of this country. I have noticed from other politicians who are looking after the power and prestige they can gain from holding office these are the kind of officials Jesus Christ was talking about when He was talking to the religious officials He said something about you brood of vipers and how they like to sit in places of honor and have people give praises to them and that's what they are all about kind of like what I see in some of these politicians who are holding office today. as I said before do you think they care a rat behind about the people they are to serve? not a chance. Once they are in office, they easily forget the people who voted for them, sure they will do minor things here and there, but what about the major issues? Like North Korea? China, trade agreements, Iran and things that threaten our sovereignty I mean the things that really matter the most to me like keeping our country safe from foreign invaders and those who would like nothing more than to ruin this great nation. Would you allow a stranger into your house and allow him to take control of your family and belongings without your invitation? then why are many liberals and democrats or whoever allowing or against building a wall? isn't this what many other Presidents talked about but did nothing. Donald Trump comes along and decides its time to keep America safe the left quickly rejects and goes on an all out war against the so called wall only because its Donald Trump nothing more, they hate the fact that he has done a wonderful job and don't want him to succeed at building this wall. If we don't protect our borders more people and law enforcement officers will be killed or wounded and some of those who will get killed might be related to you. Like myself I have a stepdaughter and her husband works to serve and protect and they both have a lovely baby boy of three years of age and I wouldn't like for my grand-son to grow up without his father the man is a great husband and father it would deeply hurt me inside if something happened to him because of some immigrant who crossed over illegally was committing a crime and shot and killed my son in law now is that fair? well brace yourself it's happening know. All this because some politicians who refused to protect its citizens, and all this because they hate Trump. **<u>"Build the wall stop the nonsense!!!!!"</u>**

Chapter Eleven

I WOULD LIKE to say that those who wanted to have Donald Trump remove from office that they concocted many false stories should be placed in prison for creating false documents and fake stories against The President of the United States to me its not any worst than the lady who decided to join ISIS and now wants to come back to the United States and pretend nothing happened it was all a mistake. No sweetheart you made that decision on your own nobody was holding a gun to your head. So, there are consequences to pay for your actions just as I paid for my stupid mistake and went to prison although I never committed the crime, but I take full responsibility. So too, those from the FBI must face their own consequences. To me I believe they thought they would never get caught or they probably thought they were above the law. And I will say it again in my opinion this was nothing more than **Treason** against the United States President. And all those involve must pay the price for their part in this nefarious act. And I'll ask again why are they not in prison for their actions? What I have seen in the lives of those who have been very adamant about ruining the reputation of a decent man and others who are for this person have nothing more than fear in their hearts and so I ask myself what is it that is tormenting them with fear? the one common denominator I come up with is fear and this fear is coming from those who have divided this nation and its in my opinion that this fear came by way of those we call the left. They have instilled all kinds of lies and false arguments that have made many people confused and troubled. The Bible says that "God did not give us a spirit of fear, but of love, power and of a sound mind" and God is also not the author of "confusion" that comes from evil entities that surrounds us. I want you to know how fearful we've become. We have become so fearful we have started to take down monuments and statutes that were erected to help us and generations to come to understand the history of this wonderful nation? and without those relics how can we teach the next generation about our history where we've been and the heart aches along the way and how this nation became a great nation, but without history we have nothing how are they going to understand and make decisions based on what they've learned of the past. The future holds nothing if we keep going in that direction. The destruction of these statues which can neither harm you or do you any good we started to get rid of them not for what they stand for but because of fear that it might harm us in some way or another but this is all a faux. Its all what we imagine in our minds that's all. They will no doubt make the same mistakes repeatedly because they have no guide into how to avoid such things. We are leaving the next generation with nothing but fear because today that is exactly what we are showing this next generation, and when fear gets a grip on you it will destroy everyone in its path. get a group of people together and put fear in that group you will see that it will slowly start to destroy each other and well in no time the group will no longer be what it was. Just remember this fear divides and a house divided will never stand. This generation is not leaving anything to hope for, if we continue in our path it is a shame to even think that the next generation not even God will be taught to those we leave behind, because we have taken God out of our lives and this is what the liberals were wanting to do so they could do as they so please, but I have news for you, you will have to answer for your evil deeds because no matter how bad you wanted to get rid of God, God is still sitting in His throne and we will have to give an account for our lives. I hope and pray that our eyes will be open and see what a mess our politicians are trying to leave us with in my lifetime. I have only seen three very strong and powerful presidents that I can recall with back bone and the names of these men are John F, Kennedy, Ronald Reagan and Donald J. Trump. this nation needs more of their kind these are the ones whom I have seen that really wanted or wants the very best for this nation and its citizens and yes you do have a right to disagree with me, because this is what freedom in our democracy is all about, let me just say what I see and hear today with those who have already chosen to run for the presidency is nothing more than a power struggle I don't think any one of those candidates are really interested in the problems of our United States and Its citizen just listen to what they stand for its all vanity, but I will put all my confidence and trust on my God and yes President Donald J. Trump as I see it God wants the very best for me and yes for you as well, God wants what's best for President Trump and this nation. The bible also tells me to pray for our leaders no matter who they are or what race, gender, or religious affiliation they might be, and It even includes to pray for our enemies so my guess is I will continue to pray for all those in office regardless of who they are, and as the elections get closer and closer we must ask God for his guidance and power to do what is right. As for me I will put my support on the one who is looking after my best interest at hand and for our God given country, that God has an eye on, so may the Lord always bless this United States of America and keep us safe from the enemies that lurk within our ranks and are trying to destroy us. It's been a little over two years since the Mueller team started this painstaking investigation as to whether President Donald Trump or his campaign committed a crime during the 2016 election by colluding with the Russian Government. now remember what colluding is. It is a secret meeting between several people in order to commit illegal activity and in this instant did President Trump met with the Russians to influence the elections or did President Trump committed obstruction of justice or simply put did The President or his administration deliberately cause the hinderance or the blockage of process from the investigation to proceed or any other legal proceedings? IF you go back to when this mess all started it was first investigated as colluding and since they couldn't get the colluding crime to stick they the "Democrats" figured The President Himself must have "Obstructed" the Investigation some how well the democrats went further than the President they started to make allegations towards anyone who was affiliated with the Trump campaign. even the Presidents cabinet members became targets and the news media took at it like it was already true and real without even getting their stories straight or at least try and verify all information that was being leaked to the media.

In Conclusion

THE ELECTIONS WERE held in 2016 and a winner was declared. This winner was Donald J. Trump a man who has made his mind up to make this nation great again and what Donald Trump committed himself to do for this great nation has been accomplished that is more character that I have ever seen displayed in a President because he has done what he promised to do. So far that to me it means a lot. This is a man of Character in my book. And for that many want to see him fail, why? he has done nothing but good for this nation. I turn to the word of God always and what I find is that evil always wants to destroy what is good. What this nation needed was a Donald Trump. I did some searching on my computer "You Tube" and what I discovered in these searches were a few things about Donald Trump that surprised me but I guess I really shouldn't be surprised, but non the less I was, and what I found out is that his vision when he was candidate Trump is still the same as it was back in the 80's when he was a guess on these talk shows. what was true then about this country is still true today. Back then Trump had not thought about running for president nor getting involved with politics. My thought about

Trump is that maybe he grew tired of all the promises that were being made by the politicians of yesteryears and never keeping their promises. and what is wrong today now this goes way back to his younger years some where along the years of 1985 or so, well anyway back in those years Donald Trump was being invited to these talk shows and he gave interviews to several talk shows and news casters. It seems to me many of these interviews were about how he saw this economy, his political views and what was his take on what was going on in the political arena, some of his interview if you'll look at them and what his opinions were at the time are basically the same, of course in those days Donald Trump wasn't thinking of running for office although many in the audience were asking him if he was thinking of running for office all he would say was something like, "That has not been on my mind". And then there were some who would tell him "You should run for President" his reaction would almost always be a little laugh and shrugged it off. Then I ask myself this question why all this animosity toward Donald Trump? It is in my honest opinion that this Presidency was already in his destiny, because for me as a believer there are no coincidences; just truth. In some of these interviews he talks about how the condition of the economy and what it really needs to turn things around and many in the audience were standing behind what he was saying. what I saw was a big approval from the audience on his ideas and thoughts. It wasn't until 1999 when Donald Trump really had this idea that maybe he should run for President. I guess he pondered on this for some time till he really decided to throw his hat in the arena. My point here is what President Trump is doing today is exactly what he was talking back in the 80's this also included immigration, border security and many things that have plagued this country since way back then. It amazes me that today as we head into another election year many on the democratic ticket have endorsed or have given some thought to make this nation a Socialist nation many have started to talk about becoming a socialist nation, what happened? Socialism has never worked and even today in this United States of America it most certainly won't work. In the coming election my vote will be for the same man who held that position four years earlier because its the only chance this nation has of surviving what those other candidates want to turn this nation into, and I faithfully believe God is not going to allow this nation to be exploited with what they think is right, because I am looking at one country who was very prosperous and growing economically and in just a few years the left have decided to go socialist they need to open their eyes and see just what happened to a prosperous country like Venezuela and see what socialism has done for them today. there is no food, money, jobs and a lot of other things this nation takes for granted. I hope and pray to the all mighty God that He continues to Bless this nation. I also pray that He would give guidance and peace to those in Venezuela that it be Gods will to heal and restore its sovereignty back to that nation, and that he looks after every one of its citizens in Jesus Holy name AMEN!!!!

We must now take a hard look at what is ahead for this nation for that we look at democratic field of candidates running for the presidency all of these candidates are really wanting to be president because they believe they can do better than what we have today but let us take a look at what we have today we have a president that really cares about our nation we have a president that has made so much progress in just a short amount of time than anyone else we have a president who has accomplish the things he said he would accomplish if he was elected president that to me speaks volumes now we look at what the democrats have accomplish with this president together NOTHING!!!!! The democrats are set in destroying our commander and chief at any cost even at the cost of this nation. The left has caused so much havoc that our President is sometime unable to do his job they say he has caused so much division among the American people but when you look at both sides I can only see the ones who are causing so much division and discord are the democrats and liberals our President has done more good for our nation. The democrats are blind or dense if they fail to see the good Donald Trump has done for our country. Today we have a robust economy, unemployment is at an all time low for many Americans whether your white, black. Hispanic or a female now that's what I call progress. When I hear the left making a statement all I hear is a negative speech. Take for instant Bernie Sanders all he talks about is making this country a socialist country giving away free stuff, and where does Bernie think this money will come from? One major source would be to raise corporate taxes but Bernie is not looking at what will happen when you start raising taxes, many companies will start laying off workers which in turn raises the unemployment rate and also many will close shop and move elsewhere again more people out of work. Then there is talk about free money for those who don't work again where is this money coming from Bernie? I mean are these candidates out of touch with reality. The democrats and liberals have got to get it together if they can. The way I look at it, all these candidates don't really care one way or the other about this country or the people. Many are talking about making this country a socialist country have they not looked at Venezuela and how that country is doing after it became a socialist county? Socialism only leads to communism. And nothing good comes out of communism. Just look at the history of what it leads too. Maybe that's what some of these candidates need to do and that is to go back to school and read up on a little bit of history. I seriously recommend this for AOC I strongly believe she has no clue what she talks about most of the times. Let's look at what a colorful list of candidates we have in the democratic line up. We have a candidate that has been accused of sleeping her way to the top of the political ladder, then there is a candidate who has been accused of being a an alleged sexual predator, whether true or not only God and they know. then we have some who have no clue as to what is really happening in this nation at all or they refuse to except the truth. Enough about the candidates lets look at the house what we have there are a bunch of democrats who could care less about this country or its people. They the democrats have done nothing but try to hinder our president from doing his job they blame Donald Trump for the division in our country when the real culprits are the democrats. What Donald Trump has done is give back to the people their dignity and selfrespect as a nation. Why would these democrats running for the presidency point fingers at our president when they themselves have issues and I mean real issues? Some of them as I said have no clue whatsoever as to how to govern a nation some lack character and integrity. Many of these candidates have being saying that Donald Trump is not fit to be president, but the way I see it neither does anyone else. The position of the highest office of this land is a very demanding position and it takes a person with courage and understanding of the issues that are affecting the people of this country and so far I hear nothing about what they intend to do about our economy, drugs, the influx of illegal immigrants coming into this country or even healthcare lets face it Donald Trump has done a marvelous job at taking on these issues and all I hear from the opposing party is "Impeachment" and I wonder what crimes has this man committed? There was an investigation of over two years and nothing came out but yet these leftist are still wanting to find something to throw at him to make an Impeachment possible come on people Hillary Clinton lost get over it and get to the real issues the people of this country have enough to worry about, than to worry about stupidity. the people of this country are smart enough to see all these accusation against our president were fabricated by dense people who don't care about this country one way or another but yet they hold very important positions in government let us not vote for these instigators once and for all. The 2020 election will be upon us lets do the right thing for this country and get rid of those who would much rather see this country in turmoil than the success this President has given us since he took office. This president cares about this country and has done an amazing job. It's to bad a president can only run for two four-year terms, do the democrats and liberals know this? I believe Donald Trump will be elected for a second term and It will be probably greater than the first term. Let the President do his job. The only thing I would say to these leftists is why oppose a good president who is doing a wonderful job of running these United States. Just a word of caution if this President is not elected for a second term, the prosperity that we have gained today will be forever lost and will not be seen again for quite sometime. This nation will be thrown into chaos and undetermined future. The present list of candidates running for the office of president have no platform to stand on and they want to destroy everything President Donald Trump has put in place. We are prospering more today than we were when Obama was President. As I look back when Obama was president I have yet to see any good thing that has come out of the Obama Administration but as I mention earlier in this writing about the money the Immigration problem and many other things were started when Obama was President not Donald Trump, Donald Trump inherited these problems from the Obama Presidency. We must all stand behind our President no matter who that person is. As I conclude my writing I will remind those who are or were confused in the beginning to sum it all up we the people have finally elected a President who has done exactly what he said he would do when he was a candidate and to me that speaks for itself. As for those who don't want to do anything to advance this great nation and create nothing but chaos I would remind you we have a duty to our country and fellow Americans we must vote those people out of office and vote those who care about this nation and want the very best for its people and to me that would be Donald Trump lets keep the prosperity going and make this a still greater nation than before thank you for reading my story,

About the Author

A little about the author I was born and raised in San Antonio Texas in the west side housing project. I graduated from Sidney Lanier High School 1977. I am a born-again Christian since the age of 12 years old we were never rich nor were we paupers my dad did the best he could to have food on the table he made sure we never went hungry even though times were tough, but thanks to God somehow we managed. We were a large family with both parents at home. Living in our neighborhood I could say we have seen just about as much violence as any housing projects are known for. Still we manage to turn out as good as we did. I am a self-educated with a love for God and music, especially music of the seventies. Growing up in the housing project was rough and filled with uncertainty at times we barely had enough to eat so by the age of eight or nine I had to work and this work included things like selling fruits and vegetables door to door or selling the local newspaper on street corners. I even had to shine shoes at a very young age in order to purchase my boy scout uniform or to pay for things like go to the movies or skating and things like that which my parents couldn't afford. I learned the value of money as I was growing up. I grew up a catholic and even went to catholic school when I was just a boy as I grew up I was also a democrat because my parents were democrats and that's all I knew I guess when your young we tend to follow in our parents foots steps when it comes to our beliefs and political affiliations. As I educated myself, I learned a lot more about God, Politics and just who I was. I accepted the Lord Jesus Christ as Lord and Savior, but life happens it was decided later in life that being a catholic was not for me I learned the history of the catholic church. In college I learned about politics and different things it was an eye opener for me I no longer wanted to be associated with the democratic party because one thing for sure in my opinion about this political party they want to keep people in slavery and bondage it is my belief as long as they can control you they can take away your dignity and self-respect and as far as I'm concern people refuse to see the truth, so I changed my affiliation and became a Republican. by this time, I had more knowledge about what both political parties stood for and made a sound decision. Well this is just a little about me as a youngster. I have decided to write a book about my life and this includes the toughest times of my life dealing with the fact that I was sexually assaulted at a very young age and dealing with alcohol and being homeless traveling from city to city never having a place of my own. Going through a divorce and how I was sentence to seven years for a crime I did not commit and how God was with me in all of life's troubles. so Again, thank you for reading my book and may my Father in heaven bless you tremendously in your life. And I hope that when you go and cast your ballot for the next commander and chief you would have had enough information to make a sound decision just as I will come Nov 2020.

www.ingramcontent.com/pod-product-compliance
Lightning Source LLC
Chambersburg PA
CBHW031523270326
41930CB00006B/500